HOW IT WAS

KNIGHTS AND CASTLES

Madeline Jones

BT Batsford Ltd, London

CONTENTS

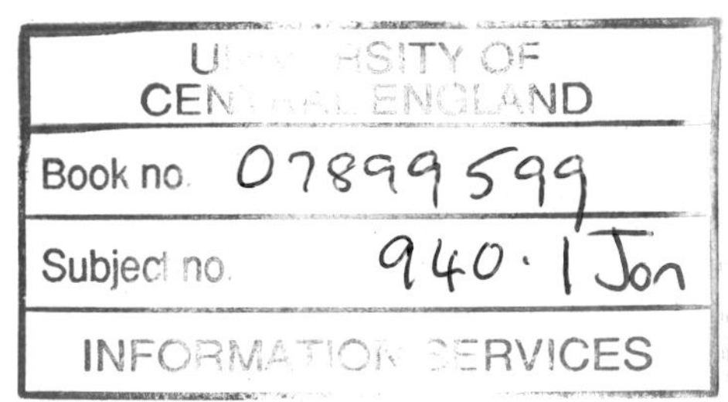

First published 1991

Reprinted 1993

Typeset by Deltatype Limited, Ellesmere Port
and printed in Hong Kong
for the publishers
B. T. Batsford Ltd
4 Fitzhardinge Street
London W1H 0AH

ISBN 0 7134 6352 X

Frontispiece: The lord of a castle like this one in France had peasants to work on his land. Can you see what they are growing? What use would the lord and his family make of this crop?

INTRODUCTION

In 1066 William of Normandy fought Harold, the last Saxon king, for the English throne. William won at Hastings, Harold was killed and the victorious Normans gradually took over the whole of England and parts of Wales. Later, they also settled in parts of Ireland and won some lands in Scotland too. They brought with them from Normandy their own customs and methods of fighting.

By 1066, castles and knights were a familiar sight in Normandy and other parts of France. At a time when kings were not strong enough to control and defend all their large kingdoms, local lords built castles, protected their own areas and fought their rivals. They made grants of land to some of the knights who fought for them and these knights became their *vassals*. A vassal paid homage to his lord, putting both hands between his lord's hands, and promising to be loyal (this ceremony still takes place at British coronations). The local lord himself did homage to the king and was the king's vassal. Like other vassals, he fought in his overlord's army when necessary. Any vassal who was disloyal or did not carry out his duties could have his lands taken away – if his overlord was powerful enough to take them. A lord had his duties too, though: he had to protect his vassals and settle any complaints fairly. If he failed to do so, the vassal could withdraw his homage and rebel – as English barons did against King John in 1215. The Latin word for land granted to a vassal is 'feudum', a fee, which gives us the word sometimes used to describe these customs – *feudal*.

Knights and their lords did not farm their lands themselves. This was done by peasants, who lived very different lives from the castle-dwellers whose food and labour they provided. Knights everywhere had more in common with each other than with ordinary people in their own districts. In England, most knights continued to speak French for centuries after 1066. They had relations and sometimes lands in different parts of France too. English kings controlled parts of France, and at times even claimed the French throne. National boundaries were not fixed as they are today.

During the years when knights and castles were important in Britain – that is, from 1066 to around 1500 – kings in England were generally more powerful than rulers were in many parts of Europe. Saxon kings had had special royal powers, and William the Conqueror made full use of these. He also gave lands to his Norman lords or barons only on strict conditions. In England, the king's permission was needed for castle-building. Even so, it was not easy to discipline a disobedient vassal once he had built one or more strong castles. Kings had to be able to make themselves obeyed. Successful kings took care to keep their barons' respect and support. They also built strong castles of their own.

Introductory quiz

Do you know

what a shell keep is?

how to undermine a castle wall?

what a portcullis is and where in a castle you would look for one?

who built Harlech Castle?

how a knight carried his lance?

anything about the Black Prince?

THE FIRST CASTLES

Most of you will have seen a castle, even if it was only from a bus, car or train. All of you will have seen pictures of castles, in books or on TV. Shut your eyes for a moment and think about castles. What do you see with your mind's eye?

You probably did *not* see anything that looked like one of the earliest castles, unless you thought of a child's pile of sand on a beach. When the Normans invaded England in 1066 they needed a lot of castles in a hurry where they could live safely while they made the Saxons obey them. They used techniques developed in Normandy to put up several hundred very simple castles. First a ditch would be dug (who do you think was made to do the digging?), then the earth from the ditch would be piled up and packed hard with stones or turf to form a mound or 'motte'. A fence of earth and timber went round the top of the motte, and a wooden building was put on the flattened space inside the fence. Another ditch and earth-and-timber barricade surrounded a large space at the foot of the motte. This was called the 'bailey'. Wooden buildings for the lord and his family and knights were set up in the bailey, with stables for the horses. The cramped space at the top of the motte was chiefly used when the castle was under attack. Then the wooden bridge or ladder linking the motte to the bailey could be drawn up or destroyed, and the motte could be defended even if enemies got into the bailey.

You can still find traces of these 'motte-and-bailey' castles today. Sometimes they form part of later stone castles, sometimes you come across them in unexpected places. Look out for large grassy mounds like the one in the picture.

This was once part of a castle. It was photographed by a school student in a park in Tonbridge, Kent.

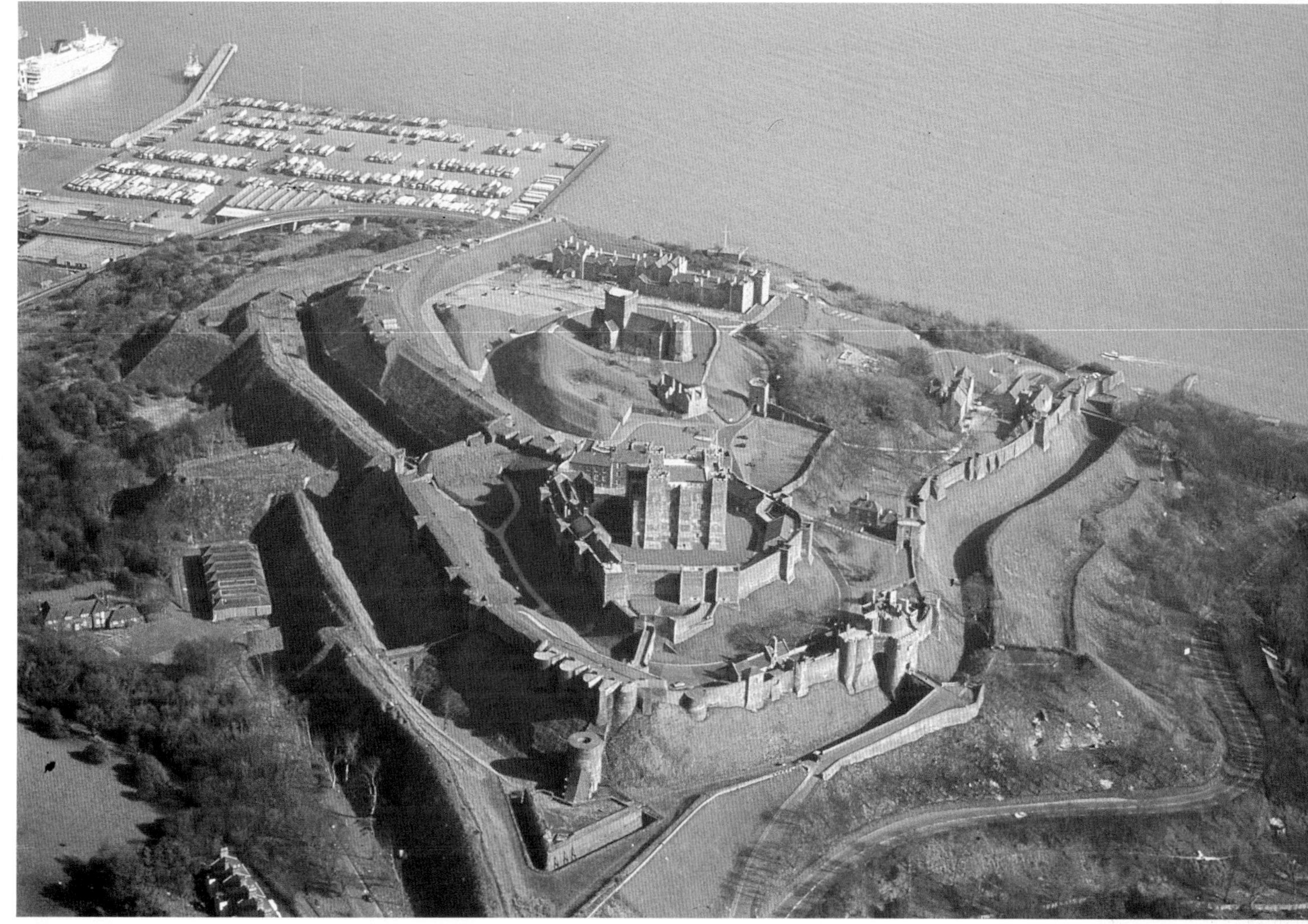

You can see Henry II's stone keep in the middle of all the later fortifications at Dover castle.

A few early castles were made of stone, like William the Conqueror's White Tower in London and his tower or *keep* (a later word for a tower) at Colchester in Essex. Stone-built castles were strong but very expensive. Henry II spent at least £1000 on a stone keep at Newcastle upon Tyne in the 1170s. This was about a tenth of his whole income for a year. At Dover, a great stone keep with walls about six metres thick and a height of nearly 30 metres cost Henry even more – £2000 in all.

If a local lord could afford to modernize, he rebuilt his motte-and-bailey castle in stone. He might put a stone keep on the motte. If the artificial mound could not bear the weight of a stone building, the new keep would be built in the bailey. Stone outer walls would also be built. Another possibility was to put a stone wall round the top of the motte, a *shell keep*, with wooden or stone buildings inside. One of the Queen's palaces has a shell keep: have you seen pictures of a royal palace which has a mound with a tower on top? Around the tower (a later building) you can see a low wall – the old shell keep. The mound rises above the rest of the palace (which is still called a 'Castle'). There is another good shell keep at Carisbrooke Castle on the Isle of Wight and others at Launceston and Restormel in Cornwall.

Not all knights lived in castles. Some just had wooden houses protected by a strong fence. They would often spend some weeks of the year in a castle belonging to their lord, though, doing 'castle-guard' or garrison duty.

THE FIRST CASTLES

We can learn about some early castles and their owners and neighbours from written accounts or *chronicles*, like the chronicle kept by the Saxons before and after 1066. This Saxon chronicle was written in old-style English, but most other writings of the time were in Latin, the language of learned churchmen, or in French. Our extracts have all been translated into modern English.

Castles and William the Conqueror

When the king was informed that the people in the north had gathered together and would oppose him if he came, he marched to Nottingham and built a castle there, and so on to York, and there built two castles, and also in Lincoln, and in many other places in that part of the country.

(*Anglo-Saxon Chronicle*, 1068)

He caused castles to be built
Which were a sore burden to the poor.

(*Anglo-Saxon Chronicle* on the death of William I, 1087)

William and his Normans would have been proud of the number of castles they had built by 1087.

How did the Saxons feel about the castle building?

(We know from William's great survey, the Domesday Book, 1086, that houses were destroyed in some places to make way for a castle: 166 houses in Lincoln, 113 in Norwich.)

Bad neighbours in bad times

Strong kings like William the Conqueror and his sons, William II and Henry I, kept their barons in order and controlled castle-building. Henry I, though, left the throne to his daughter, Matilda. Some barons did not want a woman as a ruler (can you think why?). They supported Henry's nephew Stephen instead, and there was a civil war. Between 1138 and 1145 there was disorder in some areas. William of Malmesbury, a monk from Malmesbury Abbey in Wiltshire, wrote a Latin Chronicle describing life at this time of upheaval.

There were many castles throughout England, each defending, or more properly speaking, laying waste, its neighbourhood. The garrisons drove off from the fields, both sheep and cattle . . . Plundering the houses of the wretched husbandmen [farmers] even to their very beds, they cast them into prison, nor did they free them, but on their giving everything they possessed . . . for their release.

(William of Malmesbury, *History of his Own Times*, describing events of 1140)

In what ways were the castle garrisons making a profit out of the countrypeople?

THINGS TO DO

Make a model of a motte-and-bailey castle. You'll find that a round ice-cream container makes a good mound, and you can paint a piece of paper or card to make the bailey. Don't forget to show the ditches. Modelling clay will do for the earth base for the wooden fences – you can stick twigs into it, or paint a fence on card or corrugated paper.

CAN YOU REMEMBER ?

the names of two or more towns where William the Conqueror built a castle?

CAN YOU WORK OUT ?

why the French word for a tower or keep – DONJON – turned into our word DUNGEON?

The Bayeux tapestry, an embroidery made not long after 1066, records the Norman Conquest. What is happening in this scene? Note the layers of stone and turf being used for the motte.

STRONGER CASTLES

The Norman owner of a motte-and-bailey castle would have opened his eyes wide in surprise at the sight of a castle 200 years or so after 1066. Indeed, he might not have recognized his own castle. New ideas for better defences had led kings and great lords to improve old castles and build splendid new ones.

If you visit an old castle which is still in good condition, you can trace the improvements made to its defences over the years. Look at the main entrance: is there a strong stone gatehouse? These gatehouses were popular from the thirteenth century onwards. Are there battlements along the walls, behind which defenders could hide while they shot at attackers or threw stones down at them? Battlements with crenellations (stone slabs with gaps between them) were common by the twelfth century. Are there stone towers at intervals along the outer walls, from which archers could shoot at anyone attacking the walls? Better still, are those towers round, with no corners for attackers to chip away at with a bore? Have the outer walls themselves got a slope or plinth at the bottom, to make things difficult for enemy bores or battering rams?

Goodrich Castle on the river Wye was brought up to date over several centuries. Soon after 1066 the first earth and timber castle was built (no artificial motte was needed on this rocky site). Then a rectangular stone keep was added in the twelfth century. The impressive walls and circular corner towers, and the strong gatehouse, were built in the thirteenth century. In the fourteenth century a barbican, or outer defence, was added, making it difficult for an enemy force to reach even the gatehouse.

Another castle brought up to date from time to time was Caerlaverock, on the borders of Scotland. An early castle on a mound was abandoned by the 1270s and a new stone castle built (see page 10 for a description). This castle was damaged in sieges, and part of it was even pulled down, between 1300 and 1370, but it was rebuilt and its gatehouse strengthened over the next 100 years. Fine new parapets with *machicolations* were also added: you can see these in the picture on page 10, and a diagram on page 15 will help you to understand how they worked.

Some of the best-defended castles in Britain were built new by Edward I, to hold down Wales. Edward spent about £80,000 on his eight new royal castles in Wales. Harlech Castle, which you can study in detail over the page, was started in 1283 and took seven and a half years to build. It cost about £9500 in all. Edward brought skilled workers from all over

England to work on his castles. In the summer of 1286 nearly 1000 men were working at Harlech. These men were paid, but even so not all of them wanted to work so far away from home. We know that in 1277 soldiers were paid to guard a group from Yorkshire coming to build two other Welsh castles (Flint and Rhuddlan), 'lest they flee on the way'.

Goodrich Castle had the advantage of being built on solid rock.

STRONGER CASTLES

Sometimes we can find descriptions of castles in poems or chronicles. Written royal government records (including accounts of money spent) also give us useful information.

Improving a royal castle

Henry III, father of Edward I, ordered the Sheriff of Herefordshire to repair and extend Hereford Castle in 1265. He was to:

> **fit the tower of Hereford castle with joists [beams] and roof it with lead; to make a bridge to the tower, repair the king's and queen's halls, chambers and kitchens, the larder, the knights' chambers, the king's chapel, the stable and two turrets; to finish a chamber lately begun for the king's clerks; to make a bakehouse; to repair the . . . wall round the castle and the towers in the inner bailey; and to make a building for housing engines, the gate beneath the tower, the swing-bridge there, and a prison within the castle.**
>
> **(Liberate Rolls, Henry III, quoted in J. J. Bagley, *Historical Interpretation*, Pelican, 1965)**

Can you work out from this extract the military improvements the king is having made? (You'll have noticed that he is also making the living-quarters more comfortable.)

What tells us that Hereford Castle has a keep?

You will find out more about 'engines', on page 14.

The new castle at Caerlaverock

A poem (in French) about Edward I's attack on Caerlaverock in 1300 describes Sir Herbert de Maxwell's new castle there:

> **In shape it was like a shield, for it had but three sides round it, with a tower at each corner, but one of them was a double one, so high, so long and so wide, that the gate was underneath it, well made and strong, with a drawbridge . . . And it had good walls, and good ditches filled right up to the brim with water.**
>
> ***(The Book of Caerlaverock*, 1300)**

Remember this castle had only been built in the 1270s, so it would have seemed very up to date to the writer of the poem.

What particularly impresses him?

Compare this view of Caerlaverock Castle with the written description. Do you think the castle looks 'like a shield'?

Harlech Castle

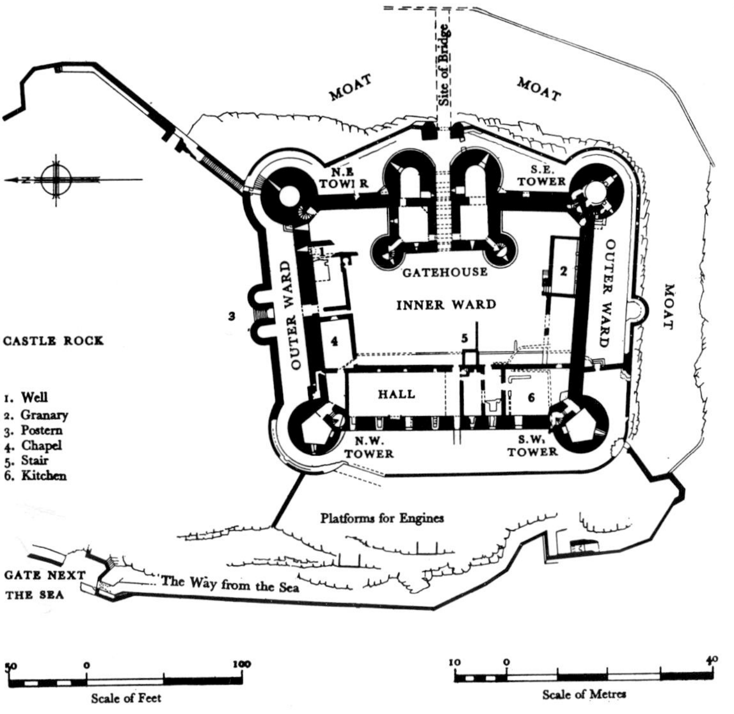

Harlech is an example of a concentric castle, that is, one with two circles of walls. Can you work out why concentric castles were very difficult to attack?

Study the plan and the photograph. Can you find:

a) the inner courtyard or 'ward'?
b) the outer ward?
c) the gatehouse?

Which part of a concentric castle like this one would be the very strongest point, replacing the old-style keep?

Look again at the picture. Why do you think Edward I chose this spot for a castle? (If you look again at the plan, you will notice that the landscape has changed since Edward's day: look at the bottom left-hand corner for a clue to show that the castle's position was even stronger when it was built than it is now.)

CAN YOU REMEMBER ?

why it was useful to build round *towers along outer walls and to make a slope at the foot of the walls themselves?*

where, as well as in Harlech, you could find Edwardian castles in Wales?

THINGS TO DO

On a large sheet of paper, mount drawings or photographs (you may be able to find old postcards or illustrated tourist brochures) to show improvements to castle defences. Don't forget to name the castles in any pictures you use, and if you can find out the date of the improvement (a gatehouse, for example), give it.

CAN YOU WORK OUT ?

Concentric is a mathematical term meaning 'having a common centre'. Can you work out why castles like Harlech are called concentric castles?

DEFENCE AND ATTACK

Usually, it was easier to defend a castle than to capture one, that is, if the castle had plenty of food and a good water supply. Anyone who built a castle where there was *not* a good supply of water was very foolish. The best thing was to have a well inside the keep (you can easily work out why that was). A sensible lord or his deputy (the castle's constable or castellan) kept a good stock of food, just in case. He also stored plenty of weapons and ammunition – arrows, bolts for cross-bows and stones for slings, which were stronger versions of our children's catapults. Large stones were kept too, for dropping through machicolations (see page 15) or through 'murder-holes' in the roof of the entry-passage leading through the gatehouse. You can see good examples of murder-holes if you visit Goodrich Castle.

Defenders of a castle needed to keep a good look-out. (When you are able to visit a castle, go to the highest point you can safely reach and look out: how much of the surrounding countryside can you see?) The first thing to be done if an enemy was spotted was to raise the drawbridge over the wet or dry moat. The main gate would be slammed shut and the portcullis (an iron grating) lowered to block the inner passage. Some later castles had more than one portcullis: Edward I's Caernarvon Castle had six.

With all these obstacles in their way, attackers often had to prepare for a long siege (the word comes from a French verb, sièger, meaning 'to sit down in front of'). They would try and stop any food getting into the castle and they would prepare 'engines' or 'machines' to attack its walls. There is a drawing of

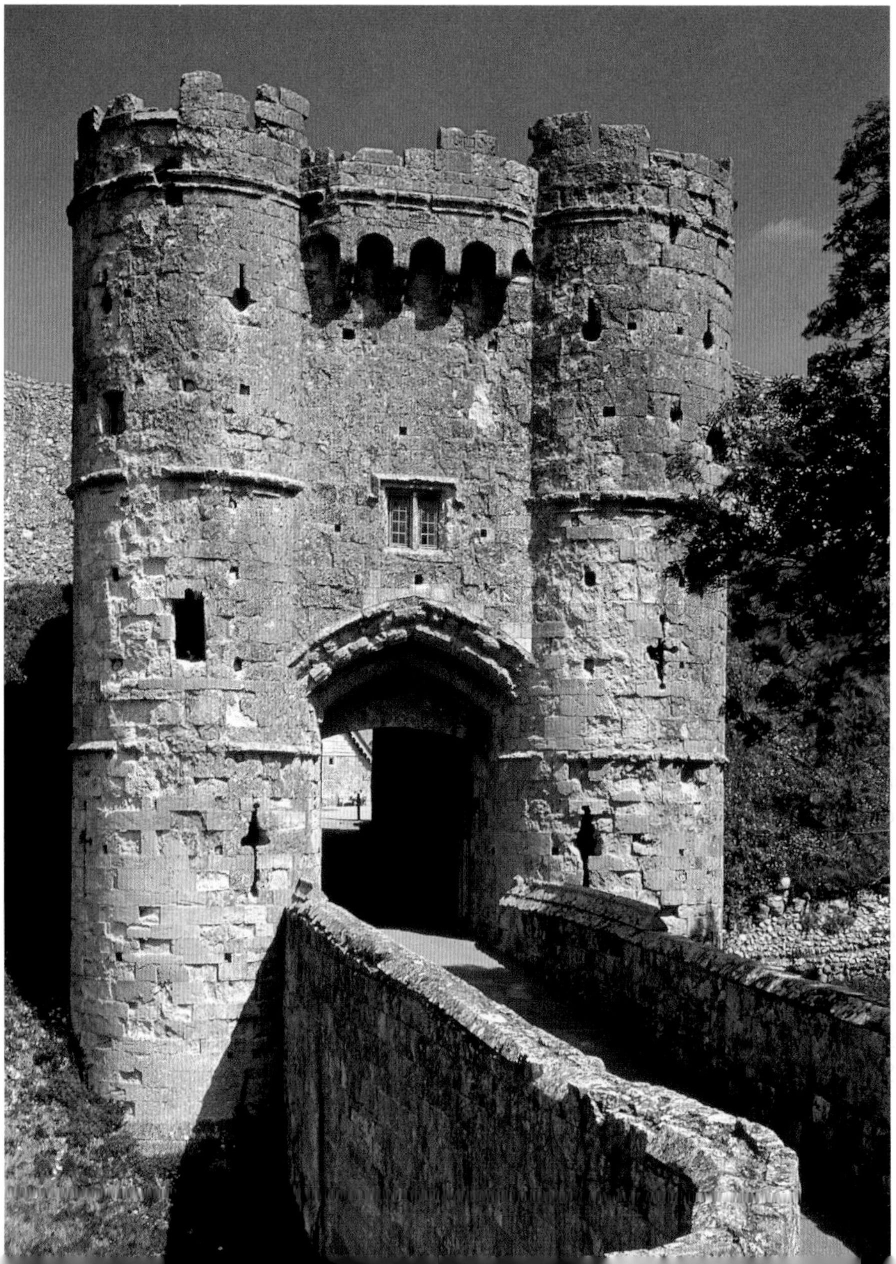

Great stone gatehouses like this one at Carisbrooke, Isle of Wight, made things difficult for attackers. Can you find the machicolations which protected the entrance? If you study the diagram over the page you will see the point of putting them there!

Kenilworth Castle once had elaborate water defences, including an artificial lake. You can see from this view that these have now disappeared. In 1266, though, the fact that the castle was almost surrounded by water made it impossible for Henry III's forces to take it by force from his sister Eleanor's son. An attempt to use boats to reach the castle failed. In the end the defenders were starved out: the siege lasted six months.

one type of 'engine' on page 14. Sometimes, tunnelling miners could make a wall collapse and then attackers would rush into the gap – 'into the breach'. Castles built on solid rock had the best defence against such mines.

Once inside the outer walls, the attackers still had a long way to go before they controlled the castle. In a concentric castle, they would have to start all over again on the second set of walls (look back at the picture of Harlech to remind yourself of this). Even in an older-style castle, they would have to get from the bailey into the keep. When King John besieged Rochester Castle in Kent in 1215, its defenders held out in one half of the keep even after the king's men had undermined and entered the other half. In the end they were starved out.

As you can see, a well-stocked castle could hold out for a long time defended by quite a small garrison. There were about 100 knights in Rochester Castle in 1215, with some ordinary soldiers, and it took King John nearly two months to capture it, in spite of his miners and five 'throwing machines'. Sometimes, though, tricks and treachery could lead to the capture of a castle. There is a sad story about Ludlow Castle on the Welsh borders in the twelfth century. A prisoner in the castle – 'a young bachelor and fair' – persuaded Marian, a waiting woman to the lady of the castle, to let him escape. Later, when the lord of the castle was away, the young man persuaded Marian to let him climb up to her. She gave in because she was in love with him and he promised to marry her. However, he left a leather ladder hanging down for his friends who climbed up and captured the castle, killing many of the guards. Marian, horrified, killed herself by jumping from a window: but first she killed the knight who had betrayed her by stabbing him with his own sword.

DEFENCE AND ATTACK

A direct attack on a castle could lead to heavy casualties amongst the attackers. Archers shot at them from arrow slits in the walls or from the battlements. The defenders often had their own 'engines' to hurl missiles over the walls on to the enemy. Men climbing the scaling-ladders brought up to the walls could all too easily be toppled off. A clever or lucky attacking force tried to take the defenders of the castle by surprise.

Sometimes castles were successfully 'stormed', that is, taken by force. Henry III took Bedford back from a disobedient vassal in 1224. After an eight-week siege the keep was undermined and the garrison captured. They were all hanged for holding out so long. More often a surrender was negotiated.

The Welsh take Abergavenny Castle in the 1180s

[The Welsh attackers] concealed themselves with a strong force of soldiery in the overgrown ditches of Abergavenny Castle . . . The previous day, one of their number . . . said to the constable as if he were warning him, but apparently more for a joke and a laugh than seriously: 'That is where we shall climb in tonight'. As he spoke he pointed to one of the corners of the wall . . . The constable and his household stayed on guard all night, refusing to take off their armour and remaining on the alert until first light. In the end, tired out . . . and feeling safe now that day had dawned, they all retired to bed. Thereupon their enemies dragged the scaling ladders which they had prepared to the precise corner of the walls . . . pointed out. The constable and his wife were captured and so were most of their men. A few escaped, finding refuge in the master tower. The Welsh occupied the castle and burned the whole place down.

(Gerald of Wales, *The Journey Through Wales*, Penguin Classics)

This chronicler, Gerald, wrote about his journey through Wales in the 1190s. He was a churchman and wrote in Latin, but he was part Norman and part Welsh.

What does his attitude to the two sides seem to be in this extract?

What lessons do you think the constable of Abergavenny should have learnt from this experience?

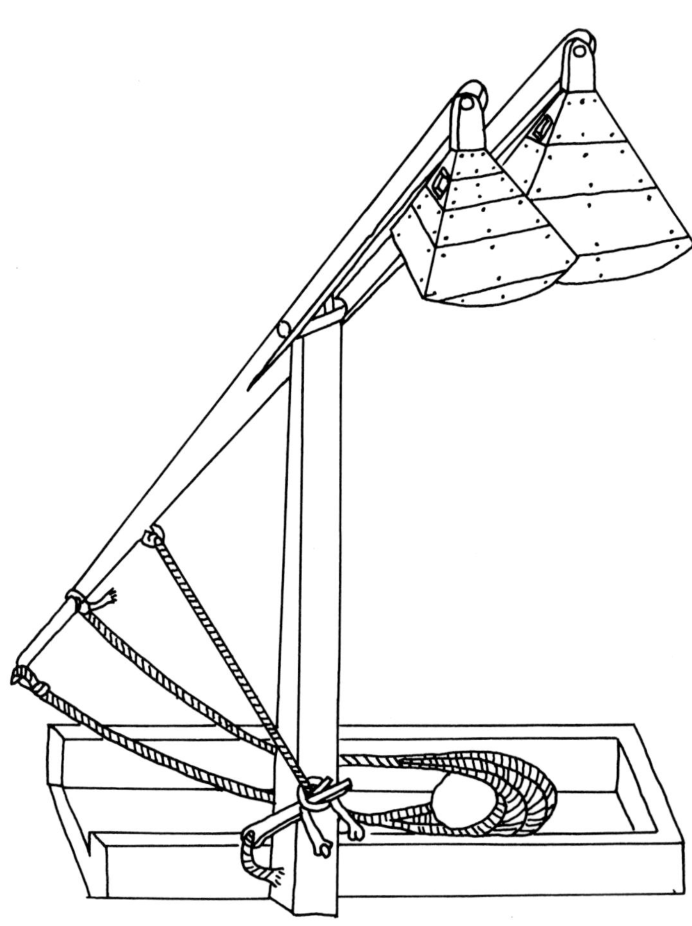

This stone-throwing 'engine' is called a Trebuchet. *It worked by means of* counter-weights. *If you do not already know how counter-weights operate, you will probably be able to work this out by studying the drawing: notice what will go down as the heavy stone goes up.*

The Black Prince captures a castle in France, 1356

The following day our men at arms crossed the moat and attacked the castle walls, which they hastened to scale with ladders while others burnt down doors; they forced their way in and killed many knights, while the two lords retreated with a number of others into the keep . . . The prince gave orders that stone-throwing machines and 'tortoises' for the protection of the miners should be built. The machines, manned by specially trained troops, destroyed the roof of the tower and the battlements with round stones. [The attackers] also set fire to the tunnel which the miners had dug and which reached to the foundations of the castle, burning the timbers which had hardly been strong enough to prevent the foundations from collapsing on the men who were digging it, and these would have fallen into the mine. But the helpless besieged saw their safety threatened by so many dangers that they begged to be allowed to surrender; and this was agreed . . . on the sixth day of the siege.

(Geoffrey le Baker's Chronicle, written about 1357–60, quoted in Richard Barber, *Life and Campaigns of the Black Prince*, The Boydell Press, 1986)

Machicolations were jutting-out parapets with holes in the floor: useful for dropping things through!

Why did the defenders of this castle have to give in?

Can you work out, or find out, what 'tortoises' were?

How could a mine make a wall collapse? (Remember what miners use to hold up the tunnel they are working in, and what happens if these are destroyed.)

You'll find out more about the Black Prince on page 26.

THINGS TO DO

Turn out the coins in your purse or pocket. You may find a picture of a portcullis, which you can reproduce by drawing or rubbing.

Imagine you are the constable of Abergavenny Castle. Tell your side of the story of the attack on the castle.

Draw a strip cartoon of the Black Prince's attack on the castle.

Use the material in this section to make a plan for an attack on a castle – then give your soldiers their instructions.

CAN YOU REMEMBER ?

who attacked Abergavenny Castle?
where the defenders of both these castles retreated to when their enemies broke in?
how to spell the word meaning 'a sit-down in front of a castle with an army'?

INSIDE A CASTLE

The outside of a deserted stone-built castle today often looks much the same as it did when it was in use, or at least you can get a good idea of how it looked. When you get inside the walls, though, it is much less easy to work out what the place was like when it was lived in. Roofs and floors may have disappeared (what material easily rots away?) and there will be no furniture left to show us what the rooms were used for. We have to look for clues in the buildings themselves, as well as finding pictures and written descriptions of castles belonging to the same period.

Earlier castles were generally less comfortable than later ones. At first, even the lord and his family had very little privacy and few luxuries. They and their guests ate in the Great Hall with the knights and castle staff, though the lord's table was on a platform at one end of the Hall. The lord, and sometimes his lady, had a chair; everyone else sat on benches along trestle tables which were taken down at the end of a meal. There were two main meals a day. Dinner was at ten or eleven in the morning and supper at about five in the afternoon. Spoons were provided but no forks, and people used their own knives. Wooden dishes called trenchers were shared by each pair.

The lord and his lady had another luxury too – a proper bed, either curtained off in a corner of the Hall or in a separate room or chamber. Everyone else slept where they could, many of them on the floor of the Hall. People often slept in some or all of their clothes, or, if they had a bed, piled cloaks on top of themselves. Rich people had fur-lined bed covers. Castles were cold places. Some early Halls did not have proper fireplaces, only a stone hearth in the middle of the floor for the log fire. Other rooms had no heating, unless a container (a brazier) with some burning charcoal was carried in.

The Hall was sometimes in the bailey, sometimes in the keep. If you visit a stone keep, you can often identify the Hall even if there are no floorboards left. Look upwards from the inside (the ground floor of a keep was usually used for store-rooms). See if you can spot a fireplace on the first or second floor: you will be able to see the slots in the walls where the floor timbers once went. Look for large windows too: these are likely to belong to the Hall. (Can you work out why most windows in a keep were kept as small as possible?)

The Great Hall at Kenilworth was built late in the fourteenth century by John of Gaunt, the Black Prince's brother. It was built in the bailey of the existing castle and was very luxurious. Notice the big windows and one of its two large fireplaces: you will see these at first-floor level, above the store-room on the ground floor.

In later castles you will find many stone buildings in the bailey, including one or more Halls with private rooms above or alongside them. The lord's family would now have a *solar*, or private sitting-room, as well as several bed-chambers. Really splendid castles like Harlech or Caernarvon (see pages 11 and 12) had several suites of rooms for grown-up members of the lord's family or important visitors. These might be in the gate-house or in the towers along the walls. Rooms became more comfortable. Many more had fireplaces, there were more beds and stools, and even more chairs. Walls were hung with cloth or leather, or lined with wood: all this made rooms warmer than in earlier days when walls were bare stone or painted plaster. There were more family possessions and wooden chests to store these in. In spite of the growing number of private rooms, however, the lord's Great Hall remained the important centre of the castle, where everyone met to eat, talk and be entertained.

In early castles even living-room windows were very small and light seeped into staircases and passages through slits designed to protect archers. This modern drawing shows how a longbowman would make use of an arrow-slit.

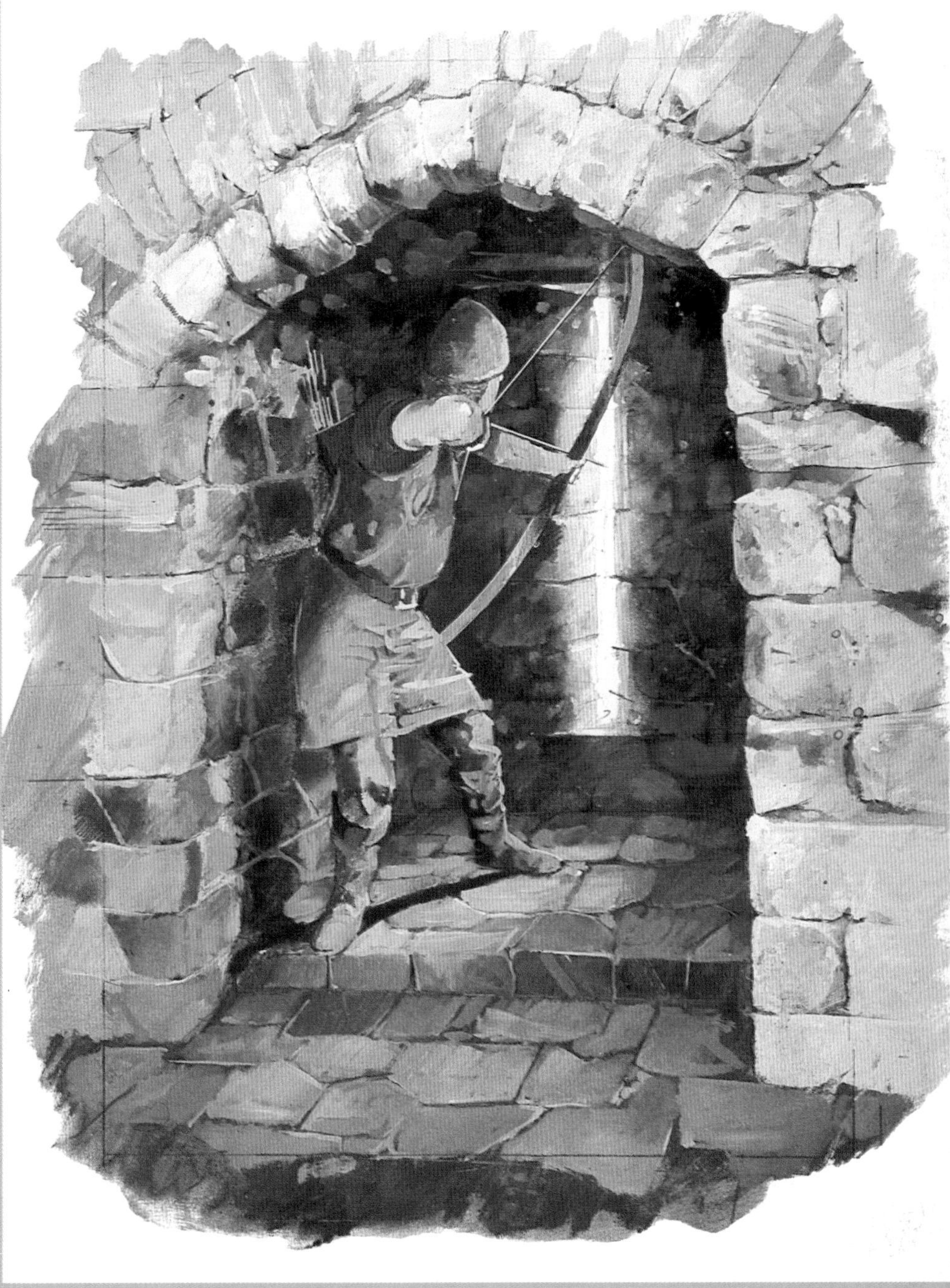

INSIDE A CASTLE

Keeping a castle reasonably clean was not easy. The floor of the Hall was often filthy as dogs scrambled about and caught (or missed) scraps thrown from the tables. There were no flushing lavatories, but only 'garderobes', small closets built into the walls of bedchambers or passages. These sometimes drained into a pit, or even into the moat. Often the servants carried away the waste. The lord and his family did have baths. These were barrel-shaped and were filled with water and then emptied by servants. Knights and ladies washed their hands before meals too. Servants had little chance to keep themselves clean.

CHECK YOUR UNDERSTANDING

What do the following words mean?

Solar

Brazier

Garderobe

Can you work out why we call the most important person at a meeting the 'chairperson' (or chairman if he is a man)?

A clean hall

Thomas à Becket, chief adviser to Henry II, and later Archbishop of Canterbury, was considered unusually careful about cleanliness.

> **He ordered his hall to be strewn every day with fresh straw or hay in winter, and with green rushes or leaves in summer, so that the host of knights who could not find room on the benches might sit on a clean and wholesome floor without soiling their precious clothes . . .**
>
> **(William FitzStephen, writing in the 1170s, quoted in *English Historical Documents II*, 1953)**

What does this extract tell you about floor-coverings for a Hall?

CAN YOU REMEMBER ?

what special luxuries lords and ladies had?

what was done to rooms in later castles to make them warmer?

what the ground floor of a keep was often used for?

THINGS TO DO

See if you can find a picture of a splendid bed with hangings or curtains to go round it. Then draw a picture of the bed that Richard II inherited from his father (you will find the 'ostrich feathers' shown on a 2p coin).

Use the information in this section and on page 10 (about Hereford Castle) to make a list of the rooms you might look for if you visited a large castle of the thirteenth century or later.

Furnishings

Edward, the Black Prince, son and heir of Edward III, had the best of everything. His will, made in 1376, lists some of the luxuries available to the extremely rich at that time.

> **We give [to Canterbury Cathedral] . . . our chamber hangings of black tapestry with a red border and swans with the heads of ladies . . . The blue clothing with golden roses and ostrich feathers we give to our son Richard, together with the bed that we have of the same suit and all the apparel [hangings, covers, etc.] of the said bed, which our father the king gave us . . .**
>
> **(Quoted in *The Black Prince and his Age*, John Harvey, Batsford, 1976)**

Why did the Black Prince have so many things decorated with ostrich feathers? (If you don't already know, see if you can find out.)

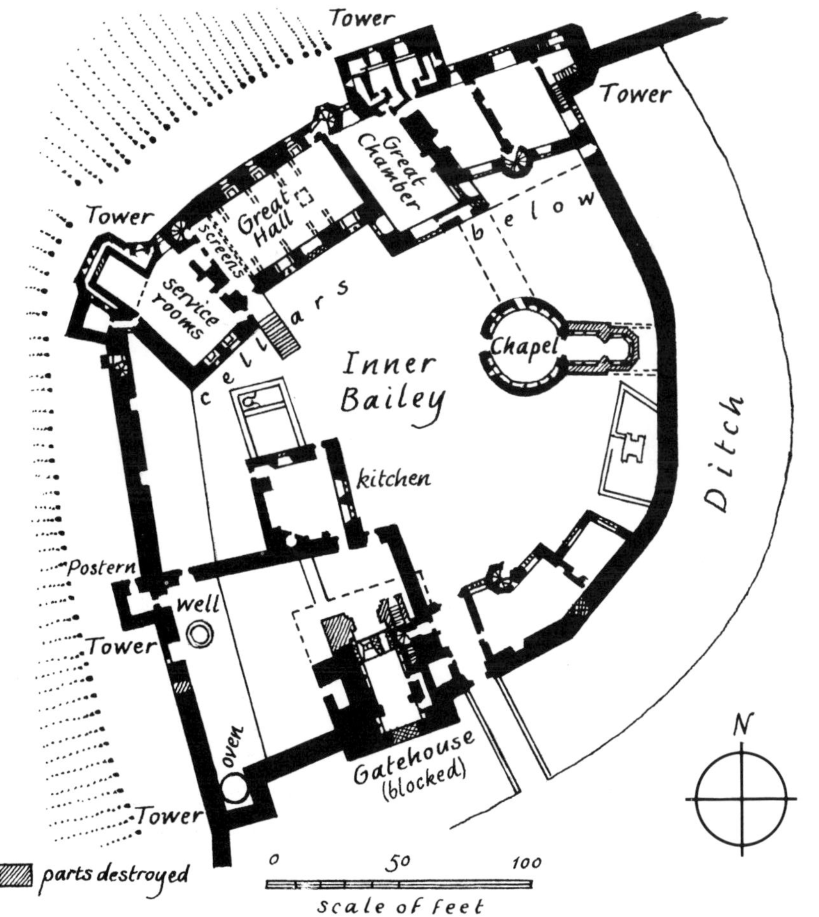

The castle at Ludlow was extended and made more comfortable around 1300. In the thirteenth century the lord and his family lived in the keep (called the gatehouse in the plan). The unusual round chapel was also in use then. Can you find the splendid new living-quarters used by the lord's family after the extension of 1300? Notice also the kitchen area and the all-important well.

DAILY LIFE

Everyone in the Middle Ages got up when it grew light and went to bed soon after dark, even people who lived in castles. It was expensive to light rooms with wax candles. Cheaper tallow candles, made from animal fat, or rush-lights, made from rushes dipped in fat, or smoky wooden torches all smelt bad and gave a poor light. In the long winter evenings, there might be some entertainment in the Hall after supper. Wandering minstrels and jugglers sang and performed, with the big fire giving extra light as well as warmth.

A French prince, the Duc de Berry, is seen here at a banquet. On the wall behind the table is a tapestry showing armed knights. Notice the dogs – and where two small ones are! What can we learn from this picture, painted around 1413, about a nobleman's life?

When the lord was at home, he would supervise his vassals and sort out their quarrels. He would consult his steward, who looked after the other servants and saw that there was plenty of food and drink in the castle. When the lord was away at the wars his lady might be left in charge. She often ran the castle and its lands very efficiently, even defending it in case of attack. In peacetime, the ladies of the castle were expected to look after the health of all the people in it. In war, they nursed the wounded. They learned how to make simple medicines from herbs.

Women were expected to have many children (it was likely some would die young from diseases easily cured today). Great ladies did not do the day-to-day child care. Each child in an important family had its own nurse. Apart from nurses and a laundress, there were few women servants in a castle. Cooks, bakers and scullions who did the dirty work in the kitchen were all men.

Older boys and often girls too were sent away from home, to relatives or to a great lord's castle. There the girls acted as companions to the lady of the castle (you will find out what the boys did on pages 24 and 25). Girls learned to spin and to embroider. Some learned to read and a few could write a little too. They listened to stories and songs, and a few ladies even wrote poems themselves. In knightly families conversation, poems and stories were mainly in French until the fourteenth century when even knights and ladies began to use English, the language of the ordinary people.

Both girls and boys played games of blind-man's buff or the quieter game of chess. Out of doors older children and men and women enjoyed hunting on horseback with packs of hunting-dogs. They liked to go hawking too, using a trained hawk to catch other birds. Animals, such as deer and birds killed by hunters and hawkers, were useful extras for the food supply. There was little fresh meat in winter otherwise, because there was little winter foodstuff for farm animals. Most were killed in November or December and their meat was salted to preserve it. This salted meat tasted so nasty after a while that spices like pepper were used to cover the bad flavour. Many recipes of the time used eggs, and fish (especially salted herrings) were popular. The Church did not allow meat to be eaten on certain days, including Fridays, so rich people ate fish instead. Some castles got fresh fish from fish-ponds outside the walls.

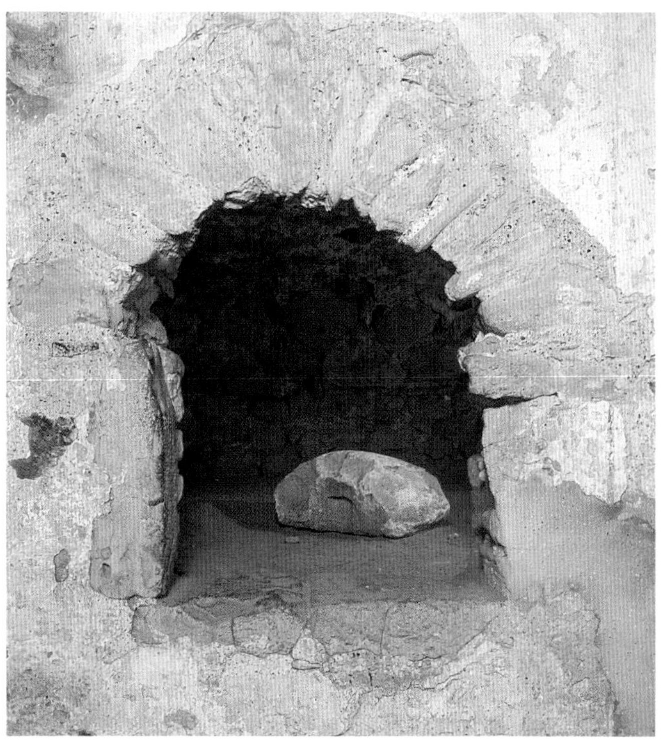

The baker, usually a man, was an important castle servant. This bread oven can be seen in the keep at Dover Castle.

Women as well as men needed to learn to ride well. Travel on horseback was quicker and easier than being jolted in a cart or even carried by servants in a litter (a kind of travelling bed). When Henry II's queen, Eleanor of Aquitaine, went on Crusade to Jerusalem with her first husband, the king of France, she rode much of the way. Ladies usually rode sitting sideways on a chair-like saddle, but Eleanor was quite ready to ride astride like a man when later in life she had to escape in a hurry.

Both lords and ladies were fond of dogs. Ladies kept small dogs as 'lapdogs'. Cats, though, were working animals, catching mice and rats. They were unpopular as pets because they were thought to be linked to witches. Pet birds and squirrels were also kept. One young girl, buried in Abergavenny, Gwent, is said to have fallen to her death from a castle wall trying to catch her pet squirrel which had escaped.

DAILY LIFE

In modern times there is plenty of material, both written and visual, to show how we live (try making your own list of sources of information for the 1990s that historians in the future will be able to use). Investigating daily life in a medieval castle is more difficult. Chroniclers and poets concentrated on what they felt were more important things (can you think what these things were?). Sometimes, though, we get glimpses of everyday life as background to their main stories.

Boys in a castle

Gerald of Wales describes some boys of the twelfth century:

> **A famous robber was being held in chains in one of the towers (of Haverfordwest Castle). Three boys, the son of the Earl of Clare, sent to Haverfordwest for his education, and two others, one of them the son of the castellan and the other his grandson . . . were in the habit of visiting the prisoner frequently. They went to him to get arrows, for he was highly skilled in fitting iron heads to them and he would give them to the boys for their bows . . .**
>
> ***(Journey into Wales*, written in the 1190s)**

One day the boys got permission for the prisoner to be let out for some fresh air. He took them hostage and bargained his release before letting them go.

How many things can you learn about boys' lives at the time from this beginning to Gerald's hostage story?

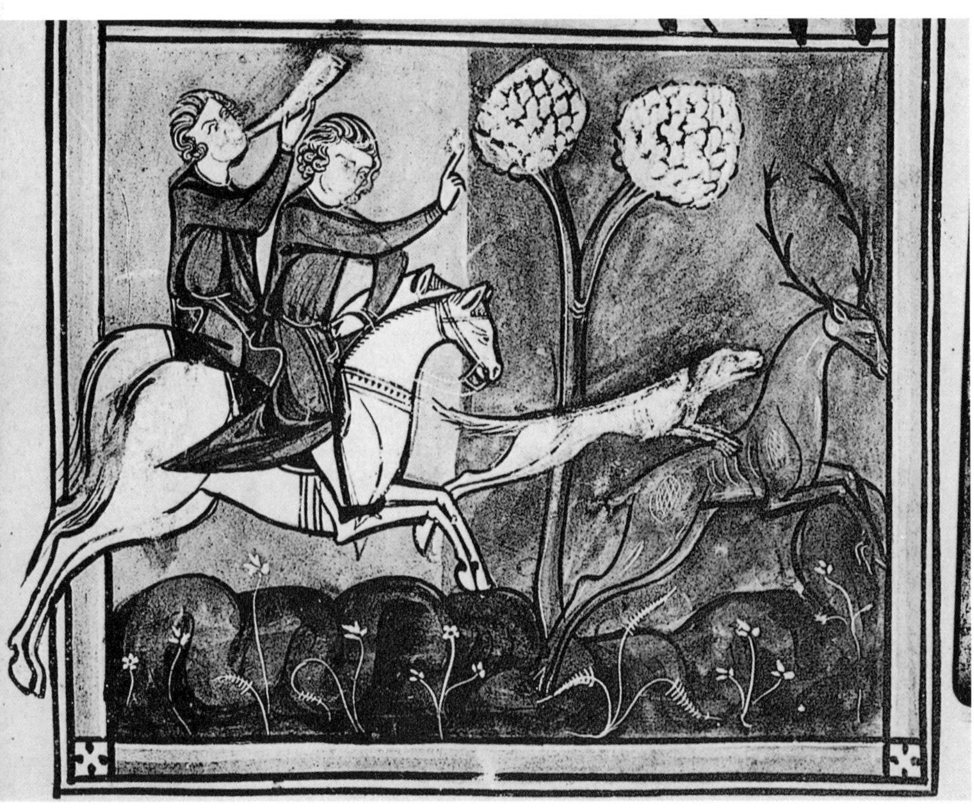

Hunting was a favourite sport for both knights and ladies.

Girls and young women

Because many royal documents, like household accounts, have survived, we can learn how princesses spent their time. In 1340, for example, more than £2 was spent on gold thread, silk and pearls for seven-year-old Joan, daughter of Edward III, for her embroidery.

Girls from noble families married young. Joan's mother, Philippa, married at 13. Her bridegroom, Edward III, was 16. Philippa was not quite 16 herself when her first son, the Black Prince, was born. She had 12 children in all: three died as babies and two more at 15. Her marriage, like those of all girls from knightly families, was arranged by her father. Like many other couples, however, Philippa and Edward grew fond of each other. She could talk him round when he was in a temper (in 1347 she did this at Calais and saved men condemned to death: you can read this famous story in Froissart's Chronicles).

THINGS TO DO

Make a study of costume in the Middle Ages, using this and other books from the library to help you. Sketch or trace a Norman lady's costume and a costume such as Queen Philippa might have worn in about 1350. What differences do you notice between the two?

Describe a day in the life of either a boy or a girl in a castle – indoors and out (you'll find more information about boys in the next section).

CAN YOU REMEMBER?

the duties of a steward?

the language knights and ladies usually spoke up until the fourteenth century?

Food and drink

Eleanor, Countess of Leicester, was a great lady, sister of Henry III and wife of Simon de Montfort, the powerful Earl of Leicester. Some of her household accounts have survived. In April 1265 she was visited at the castle of Odiham by two of her sons. Her steward stocked up:

> **Grain, 6 bushells . . . Wine, 3 sesters. Ale . . .**
>
> ***Kitchen* ½ ox from the castle stores. 1 sheep and 1 calf, 3s 3d. Hens . . . 500 eggs, 17½d.**
> **Milk 1d**
>
> ***Stable* Hay for 36 horses, from stores. Oats, 2 quarters 5 bushels from the constable's store. Sum [spent] 4s 9½d**
>
> **For the dogs of Sir Henry de Montfort and Sir Guy for the 9 preceding days: grain, 3 quarters for 46 dogs.**
>
> **(Quoted in M. W. Labarge, *A Baronial Household of the 13th Century*, 1965)**

Which provisions were kept in store in the castle and which had to be bought?

Why do you think the young men brought so many dogs?

A KNIGHT'S TRAINING

Boys of knightly rank started early to learn certain skills. Even boys who were going to become churchmen learnt to ride and to exercise with toy swords. Gerald of Wales, who spent his boyhood at his father's castle of Manorbier on the coast of Pembrokeshire, remembered in later life how he had played on the beach at being knights with his brothers. They went on to train for war, while Gerald was sent to the Abbey of St Peter in Gloucester to study for a career in the church.

You will remember that older boys were sent away from home to continue their training. It was thought they would become tougher and more independent in another household. They went at the age of about eight, to a relation (often an uncle) or to their father's overlord. Young William Marshal, who became famous enough for his life-history to be written, was sent in the twelfth century from England to a cousin's castle in Normandy: there he became, as he grew up, first a squire and then a knight. Such boys and their 'fosterfathers', the lords of the castles where they were sent, often grew very close. One writer tells us how a boy called Fulk, from the Shropshire castle of Whittington, was sent off to Ludlow Castle when he was only seven. Sir Joce, the lord of Ludlow, brought him up, and when Sir Joce was in danger during a battle outside Ludlow, Fulk saved his life. 'Fair son', said the grateful Sir Joce, 'blessed the day that ever I nourished you'. Soon a marriage was arranged between Fulk and Hawyse, daughter of Sir Joce and heiress to half his lands: she and Fulk had of course played together as children at Ludlow.

At first, youngsters like William and Fulk learnt to wait on their lords as pages. They would serve him at table and hold bowl and towel for him to wash his hands. They learnt good manners and, partly from hearing songs and stories about great knights and their deeds, they learnt what was expected of a good knight – bravery, for example, and loyalty to his lord. They learnt to sing themselves, to entertain the ladies of the castle (later, William Marshal would sing to the ladies before going to fight in a tournament) and from about 1300, most boys also learnt to read. By that time, many castle families kept a teacher for the children. Boys also learnt to handle weapons and to hunt.

In their teens, the boys served their lords as squires, helping with armour and horses (a squire led the knight's great war-horse when its owner was peacefully riding a small horse, a palfrey). The young squires practised with swords and lances. Fighting with a lance was difficult. The heavy lance had to be 'couched', or carried, under the right armpit while the rider managed his reins and his shield with the left arm – the lance was about three metres long too.

Squires longed for the day when they would be 'dubbed' knights. Royal princes like the Black Prince were often knighted at around 16. A poor squire like William Marshal had to wait until he was 20. The word 'dub' comes from the French word 'adouber', to strike a blow. An older knight would hit the young man he was knighting: this punch, or tap with a sword, showed that the youth had become a man and a knight. Knighting ceremonies varied, but the new knight always had a sword buckled round him and spurs fixed to his heels (we still use the expression 'to win his spurs').

Sometimes squires were knighted just before a battle, which made them very eager to distinguish themselves by fighting bravely. Sometimes, squires who had been especially brave in battle were given knighthood afterwards as a reward (a squire often carried his lord's banner in battle). At times, though not often, men who had not been born into knightly families were also rewarded in this way. In peacetime, young men were knighted at a church ceremony and spent the night before praying in a church.

A young knight had to equip himself with horse and armour (in this thirteenth-century painting, the armour is chain-mail). Notice the heavy helmets: sometimes these were battered out of shape and then the knights had to find a blacksmith to get them off.

el. xv. eime iour dou mois li vaillans

A KNIGHT'S TRAINING

Young knights were eager to prove their courage, both in tournaments (which you will read about in the next section) and in war. The eyes of their elders were on them: older people always like to see how the next generation is coming along!

The Black Prince's first battle

In 1346, Edward III fought a French army at Crècy. He let his young son Edward play an important part.

> **In this desperate battle, Edward of Woodstock, the king's eldest son, aged 16, displayed marvellous courage against the French in the front line, running through horses, felling knights, crushing helmets, cutting lances apart, avoiding the enemy's missiles; as he did so, he encouraged his men, defended himself, helped fallen friends to their feet and set everyone an example . . .**
>
> **(Geoffrey le Baker's Chronicle, quoted in Richard Barber, *Life and Campaigns of the Black Prince*)**

Young knights could make mistakes. The same chronicler, describing how the French actually rode over their own cross-bowmen in this battle, writes:

> **Foremost in such rashness and boldness were newly made knights, of whom there were a good number in the army, all eager to gain the glory . . .**

Prince Edward was later nick-named the 'Black Prince' from the colour of his armour.

What qualities in the Prince does this chronicler admire?

CHECK YOUR UNDERSTANDING

What do these words mean?

To dub

Palfrey

Tabard

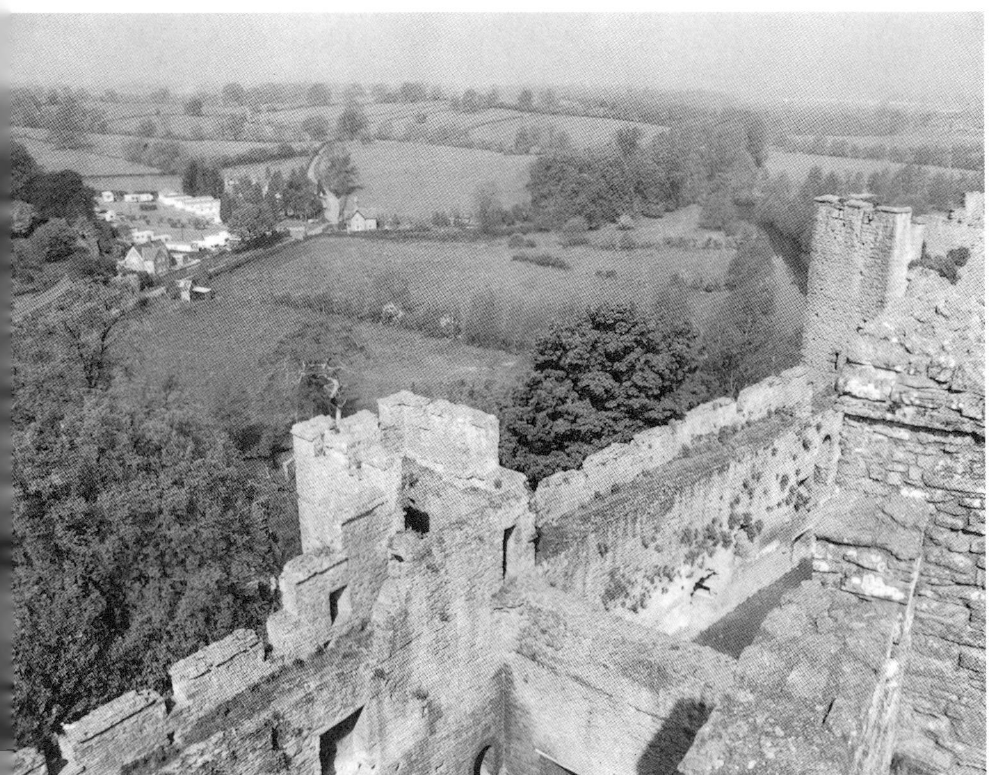

These are the battlements of Ludlow Castle. You can imagine boys like Fulk learning to walk confidently along the narrow path. Notice the good view of the surrounding country.

Advice to young knights

Young men, then as now, loved to dress smartly. Older knights often shook their heads over new fashions. Joinville, a French knight who as an old man wrote a life-history of his lord, Louis IX of France, was not afraid to tell a later king, Louis's grandson, how to dress:

> **He (King Louis) often said that people ought to clothe and arm themselves in such a way that men of ripe age would never say they had spent too much on dress or young men say they had spent too little. I repeated this remark to our present king when speaking of the elaborately embroidered tabards [tunics worn over armour] that are in vogue today. I told him that, during the whole of our voyage oversea, I had never seen such embroidered tabards, either on the king or on anyone else. He said to me that he had several such garments, with his own arms [coat of arms, see page 31] embroidered on them, and they had cost him eight hundred livres . . . I told him that he would have put his money to better use if he had given it to God, and had his clothes made of good plain taffeta bearing his arms, as his father had done.**

(*The Life of St. Louis*, written in 1309 by Joinville, translated by M. R. B. Shaw, Penguin, 1963)

Pages and young squires were expected to play chess with the ladies of the castle.

How would you describe the way Joinville speaks to the king?

(It was good manners for any knight, however important, to listen politely to an older knight.)

CAN YOU REMEMBER ?

why young boys were sent away from home to be trained?

how a lance was held?

what a squire's duties were?

how we get our expression 'to win his spurs'?

THINGS TO DO

Make up some short scenes to show the life of a page: you could start with the boy leaving home. You could mime these and get other people to tell you what was happening in each scene.

Write down some advice from an older knight to a newly-made knight. (Remember you might want to tell the young knight how to behave both in peace and in war.)

TOURNAMENTS

In peacetime, a young knight who wanted fame set out to take part in a tournament. These organized mock-battles became popular from around 1100. At first, most took place in France but soon other countries had their own tournaments.

The early tournaments were team events. When one was planned, messengers would spread the news and local lords would gather their knights together. Once at the place set aside for the contest, friends and lords from the same area with their bands of knights would group together. Individual knights would join a group and two sides would form. The tournament began with the two sides falling on each other to fight as if in a real battle. The fighting often took place over a large stretch of countryside (one English tournament was fought out between Warwick and Kenilworth in the Midlands) and might last several days.

There were very few rules at first, though the aim was to capture your rival, not kill him. However, fatal accidents did happen. A captured knight had to pay a ransom of money or give up his valuable horse, and sometimes his armour too, to the knight who defeated him. A successful champion had a lot to gain. The young and poor William Marshal started his rise to wealth and power by winning at tournaments. He made a bad start by losing his own horse in his first tournament, but those who lost horses were allowed to fight on foot and William soon replaced his by defeating another knight. In just one later tournament he won 12 horses. He had a special war-cry – 'God to the aid of the Marshal!' – which he shouted at the beginning of a fight. His rivals must have felt that God always answered his call.

By the late thirteenth century, tournaments were better organized. Contests or jousts between individual knights took up more of the time, eventually replacing the general battle. Judges kept watch and gave a prize to the 'man of the match'. Safety precautions increased. A barrier kept the two contestants' horses apart in the lists [the tournament ground] so that they could not charge into each other. Special weapons, with blunt points, were made, called arms 'à plaisance' (can you work out or look up the meaning of this French word?), for use in tournaments, in order to keep casualties down. Spectacle became more important, with processions and evening banquets. Heralds in fine costumes supervised the events. Ladies watched and encouraged their favourite champions, giving them a scarf or a loose outer sleeve from their dress to wear in their helmets. Despite these changes, tourneying [fighting in a tournament] remained a dangerous

sport. To the knights taking part, it was a useful substitute for war. For landless knights, younger sons like William Marshal who would not inherit their father's estates, it could also be a useful source of income.

In later tournaments individual knights jousted with each other.

TOURNAMENTS

The church tried to ban tournaments – you will understand why! In 1130 Pope Innocent II condemned them as:

> **'Those detestable markets and fairs, vulgarly called tournaments, at which knights are accustomed to assemble, in order to display their strength and rash boldness.'**
> **(Quoted in *The Pelican History of Medieval Europe*, Maurice Keen, Penguin, 1969)**

Henry II forbade them in England. He did not want knights to waste their energies, or their lives, in tournaments instead of fighting in the king's wars. Henry's sons went off to France to take part in tournaments though (and one, Geoffrey, was killed at one). Richard I, another of Henry's sons, enjoyed tournaments and allowed them in England when he became king. He felt his English knights needed the training they provided. He also charged those who took part. A landless knight had to pay two marks and a knight with land four marks.

Chroniclers and storytellers show us what was regarded as sporting and unsporting conduct in tournaments.

A generous gesture

Young Fulk de Warren (son of the Fulk mentioned on page 24) is said to have jousted before the king of France early in the thirteenth century. His opponent was Sir Druz, 'a very proud Frenchman'.

> **And Fulk and Sir Druz spurred their steeds, and encountered one another, and Fulk struck him with his lance through the middle of his shield, and pierced his good hauberk [coat of mail] and through the middle of his shoulder, and the lance flew in pieces. And Sir Druz fell all flat on the ground. And Fulk took his horse off Sir Druz and he led it away, and sent it as a gift to Sir Druz, for no wish had Sir Fulk to keep the horse.**
> **(*The History of Fulk fitz Warren*, a romantic story written in the fourteenth century by an unknown author)**

A good joust, 1390

This account of a joust was recorded by Froissart, who was writing from about 1370 to 1400. He was a servant of Queen Philippa, the Black Prince's mother, in the 1360s.

> **The two knights spurred forward and met this time with straight lances, hitting each other clean and hard on their shields. Both were nearly knocked to the ground, but they gripped their horses with their legs and stayed on . . . This joust was very highly applauded and both French and English said [they] had jousted admirably, without either sparing themselves or causing each other other an injury.**
> **(Froissart, *Chronicles*, translated from the French, Penguin Classics, 1968)**

Foul play, 1390

> **The Bohemian knight [Hans, one of the Queen of England's bodyguard] struck a foul blow . . . for he struck my lord Boucicaut's helm with an ugly sideways thrust . . . The English saw clearly that he was at fault and knew that he had forfeited his horse and armour if the French insisted on it . . . [the French, sportingly, did not insist].**
> **(Froissart, *Chronicles*)**

Can you see anything in the first of these two passages by Froissart to suggest that attitudes were a little softer in 1390 than at the time of Sir Fulk's fight with Sir Druz?

Heraldry

Knights in armour with helmets covering their faces could not be recognized. You can see from the picture on page 29 and from the following extract how contestants in a tournament (or in a real battle) were identified.

> **. . . Do you see that other [knight] who has an eagle and a dragon painted side by side on his shield? That is the son of the king of Aragon . . . And do you see that other one beside him? . . . bearing a shield with a leopard painted on a green ground, on one part, on the other azure blue? That is Ignaures . . .**
>
> **(Chretien de Troyes, writing 1165–1185)**

'Coats of arms' like these decorated tunics or tabards as well as shields. Officials called heralds were made responsible for keeping lists of individual and family coats of arms. There is still a College of Heralds doing this today.

CHECK YOUR UNDERSTANDING

Heraldry has its own special language. Some useful words are: or (gold), argent (silver), gules (red), azur (blue), sable (black), gryphon (a monster with an eagle's head and wings and a lion's body and legs).

'Quartering' means dividing a shield into four, to show various coats of arms inherited by the owner.

CAN YOU REMEMBER ?

what happened to William Marshal at his first tournament?

the difference between early tournaments and later ones?

THINGS TO DO

Froissart describes the arms of Hans, the Bohemian knight, as 'argent, three gryphons' feet sable with azure claws' (the first colour gives the background of the shield). Draw Sir Hans' shield with the coat of arms, and colour or paint it.

Then make up a coat of arms for yourself and draw and describe it (pictures on pages 29 and 37 will give you more ideas).

Make up a dialogue between an older and a young knight, attacking and defending tournaments.

Or make a list of rules for knights in tournaments, including things they should and should not do. Give a date (Why is this important?).

KNIGHTS AT WAR

Knights were trained to fight. They expected to ride to war from time to time, following their lords to defend their lands or to win new lands, as the Normans did in England and then in Wales and Ireland.

A knightly vassal owed his lord at first 60, later 40 days military service a year, but very soon kings in England began to pay a wage even to the knights in their armies. It was more convenient to be able to keep them after the 40 days were up. Knights unable or unwilling to fight in person paid a fine called scutage instead. A knight provided his own horse and armour, though the king might replace warhorses killed in battle. Some knights wandered from place to place, hiring themselves out as mercenaries to lords raising armies. 'I can help you. I have already a shield at my neck and a helmet on my head . . . Nevertheless how can I put myself in the field without money?', the French mercenary Bertrand de Born asked the count of Poitiers in the twelfth century.

Knights hoped to make a profit out of warfare. Captured enemy knights had to pay a ransom for their release. The more important the captive, the larger the ransom: at the battle of Poitiers (1356) the English were lucky enough to capture the French king. An enormous sum had to be paid for his freedom. Knights therefore tried to unhorse or

wound an enemy rather than kill him – unless he was too poor to pay a ransom.

Battles meant booty too. After a victory, the enemy's baggage and tents were seized. An invading army looted as it went, taking farm animals, villagers' property, townsmens' wealth. Warfare might have been a kind of dangerous game to the mounted knights but it was a tragedy for the ordinary people in the lands where the knights fought.

Knights formed the cavalry in medieval armies, using their own weight and that of their horses to batter down the enemy. In hand-to-hand fighting they used their lances and swords. Sometimes, they dismounted and fought on foot. They did not fight alone though: there were ordinary foot-soldiers or men-at-arms in the armies too. Archers were very important. From William I's time they helped to win victories. At first, they used shortbows but soon Welsh archers were recruited. They used the longbow, which shot further and more accurately than the shortbow.

Knights fought for wealth and for fame. Sometimes, they also hoped to save their souls by fighting for the Church. In 1095, Pope Urban II preached the First Crusade, or war of the Cross (the Latin word for cross is *crux*). Knights were urged to go to the Eastern Mediterranean to help Christians there against the Muslim Turks. They also wanted to recapture Jerusalem from the Turks, and this they achieved in 1099. Some Western knights stayed in Palestine and seized lands and even kingdoms for themselves. Some joined special Military Orders, giving up their lives to fighting for the Church: there was an Order of the Temple (the Templars) and an Order of St John of the Hospital (the Hospitallers). The wars in the East were as brutal as the wars in Europe and the Crusaders often persecuted and killed local Christians as well as Muslims. The great Muslim leader Saladin won back Jerusalem in 1187, and though there were many later Crusades, none was as successful as the First Crusade.

This view (on the left of the Battle of Agincourt (1415) was painted later in the fifteenth century. Can you find the royal coat of arms of the king of France? (You need to look for the golden Fleur de Lys – the lily flower.)

Compare this fourteenth-century battle scene with the Agincourt picture. You will notice differences in the armour. Do you also notice any difference in the way war is portrayed? Which picture seems to you the more realistic?

KNIGHTS AT WAR

Poets and chroniclers tell plenty of tales of battles. Some were present at the battles they describe, as Jordan Fantosme was when the English captured King William of Scotland in 1174 – 'He was soon taken, with my two eyes I saw it'. Sometimes, they depended on older chronicles, or on accounts by those who had been there in person. We cannot always tell if details are accurate. Casualties on the enemy side are sometimes suspiciously high! However, we can learn a lot about what people of the time admired, as well as getting a good general idea of what battles were like.

Two views of war

a King Edward sees them [the Scots] coming down the meadow,
He shouts to his barons, 'Let us advance in God's name!
Then earls and barons spur their steeds;
He who can run quickest goes into the battle.
The knights on the other side who were mounted,
When they see the banner of Edward the wise
With the three leopards displayed in the field,
Now fled and left without aid
All their footmen, have abandoned and lost them.
The army of the common soldiers was now severed
By the power of the English, who had no mercy;
Like flies died there a hundred thousand by sword blows . . .

(Chronicle of Peter Langtoft 1297–1307, quoted in *English Historical Documents* III)

b As an added misery, it never stopped raining the whole week and consequently their saddles, saddle-clothes and girths became sodden and most of the horses developed sores on their backs. They had nothing to cover them with except their own surcoats [loose outer robes] and no means of reshoeing the horses which needed it. They themselves had nothing to keep out the wet and the cold except their tunics and their armour, and nothing to make fires with except green wood, which will not stay alight under rain.

(Froissart, based on an earlier chronicle by Le Bel)

Both these extracts describe episodes from the wars between the English and the Scots, the first under Edward I, the second under the young Edward III, his grandson. In (b), the English knights had lost track of the Scots and were wandering about in the hills with very little food.

Which kind of warfare do you think most young knights saw themselves as taking part in?

What do you notice about the fate of the Scottish foot-soldiers in (a)?

Booty taken by the English after the Battle of Poitiers, 1356

. . . All who took part in that glorious battle under the Prince became rich in honour and possessions, not only because of the ransoms but also thanks to the gold and silver which they captured. They found plate [dishes] and gold and silver belts and precious jewels in chests crammed full of them, as well as excellent cloaks, so that they took no notice of armour, arms or equipment . . .

(Froissart, *Chronicles*)

Notice that the English were able to pick and choose what they took. What did they leave behind?

THINGS TO DO

Draw, or make out of coloured paper, Edward I's banner with the 'three leopards' of England. (You'll find a picture of them on page 32.)

See if you can find out about different kinds of armour. What type of armour would Edward I have worn in the early fourteenth century? You will be able to study the Black Prince's armour from the picture on page 36.

CAN YOU REMEMBER ?

who lost the Battle of Poitiers – and the booty? (You will probably have worked out already who 'the Prince' was: but if you haven't done this, you'll find the answer on page 38.)

This brass of around 1410 shows Sir Robert de Frevile (died 1393) and his wife Clarice (died 1399) and is in the church of Little Shelford, Cambridgeshire. There are memorial brasses of knights, and ladies too, in many old churches. What information can a brass like this give you? Sometimes, with permission, you can make your own brass-rubbing. There are brass-rubbing centres in some places: the one in the crypt (cellars) of St Martin's-in-the-Fields church in Trafalgar Square, London, has good examples of knights' brasses.

CHIVALRY

A knight was a 'chevalier' – a man with a 'cheval', a horse. He was ideally expected to live up to a knightly code of behaviour, the code of chivalry. We still use the word 'chivalrous' today. Can you think of any action you might describe as 'chivalrous'?

One set of rules of chivalry, or knightly 'courtesy' (another word we still use) developed to encourage knights to behave well to women. Poets called troubadours wrote songs and stories of knights serving the ladies they loved, sometimes saving them from danger or doing heroic deeds as proof of their love. Most troubadours were men, but a few were women, and many women, like Henry II's Queen Eleanor, Duchess of Aquitaine in the south of France, encouraged them. At Eleanor's court in Aquitaine, young knights not only heard and learnt to sing the troubadours' songs but also took part in debates with ladies over the rules of love. This 'courtly' love was a kind of game. At a time of arranged marriages, which might be just business arrangements, it added some romance to life. Slowly, though, ideas of courtly love helped to soften the hard, warlike image of the knight.

Another set of rules laid down how knights ought to behave to each other. A knight had to keep his word: if he surrendered in battle, he must not then try to escape. A good knight was generous to a defeated enemy. He was loyal to his lord and to his friends. He fought fairly – one against one – and did not cheat. However, such rules only applied to other knights. Ordinary soldiers and ordinary people were outside the code of chivalry. The Black Prince, admired for chivalrous acts (see page 38), allowed 3000 men, women and children to be killed at Limoges, a French town which he took by force. Even his admirer, Froissart, wrote of this, 'There is no man so hard-hearted that if he had been in Limoges on that day, and had remembered God, he would not have wept bitterly . . .' Normally chroniclers took for granted the sufferings of the ordinary people. 'The noble and gentle prince . . . made a fine beginning as a knight. He made a raid across the Cotentin [a district in France], burning everything and laying waste . . .' wrote a biographer of the Black Prince about the boy's first campaign in 1346.

Ideas of chivalry were linked to stories and poems about knightly deeds. Stories about King Arthur and his Knights of the Round Table were popular, especially from the late twelfth century on. The real Arthur had lived centuries earlier, and we know very little about him. Many legends had grown up about him, however, and he was thought of as a great hero.

The Black Prince seemed to English knights to be a good example of chivalry. His tomb in Canterbury Cathedral shows all his knightly equipment and is decorated with his coat of arms.

Later kings liked to be compared with him: Edward I held a Round Table tournament at Nefyn, in North Wales, in Arthur's honour (there were and still are many places associated with Arthur in Wales). Edward III went even further, making Windsor Castle the centre of celebrations in honour of Arthur and encouraging the belief that the original 'Round Table' had been at Windsor. Edward III created his own brotherhood of knights too – the Order of the Garter. You can visit the special chapel of the Knights of the Garter (St George's Chapel) at Windsor Castle, and see the banners of all the present knights hanging there.

A perfect knight was polite and protective to ladies. Here a wife and daughter arm a knight for the wars. This family, the Luttrells, lived in Somerset in the fourteenth century. They were, as you can see, very proud of their coat of arms: in how many places in the picture can you find it?

CHIVALRY

One of the aims of the chroniclers was to provide examples of knightly behaviour for future generations to copy.

Treatment of a defeated enemy

William of Malmesbury described his hero, Robert of Gloucester, capturing King Stephen at the Battle of Lincoln, 1141.

The king, though he by no means wanted [lacked] spirit to defend himself, being at last attacked on every side by the earl of Gloucester's soldiers, fell to the ground by a blow from a stone; but who was the author of this deed was uncertain. Thus, when all around him were either taken or dispersed, he was compelled to yield . . . and become a captive. On which the truly noble earl of Gloucester commanded the king to be preserved uninjured, not suffering him to be molested, even with a reproach; and the person whom he had just before fiercely attacked . . . he now calmly protected . . .

(*A History of his Own Times*)

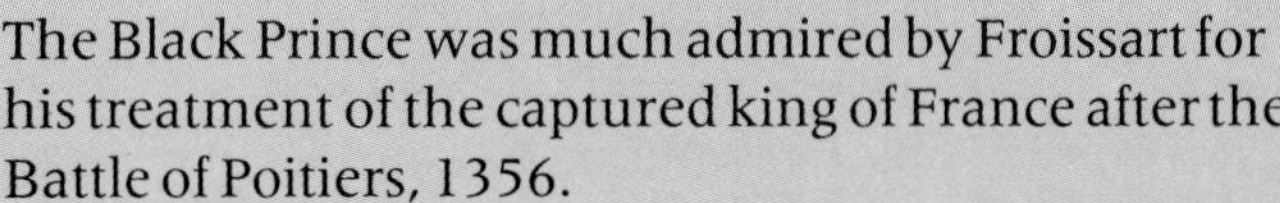

The Black Prince was much admired by Froissart for his treatment of the captured king of France after the Battle of Poitiers, 1356.

That evening the Prince of Wales gave a supper for the king of France and most of the captured counts and barons . . . He himself served in all humility both at the king's table and at the others, steadfastly refusing to sit down with the king in spite of all his entreaties . . . He [the Prince] constantly kneeled before him, saying 'Beloved Sire, do not make such a poor meal . . . In my opinion, you have good cause to be cheerful, although the battle did not go in your favour, for today you have won the highest renown [fame] of a warrior, excelling the best of your knights . . . everyone on our side, having seen how each man fought, unanimously agrees with this and awards you the palm and the crown, if you will consent to wear them'. At these words all those present murmured their approval, French and English remarking to each other that the Prince had spoken nobly . . .

(Froissart, *Chronicles*, Penguin, 1968)

In what ways did the Black Prince show courtesy to the King of France?

Why do you think both the prisoners in these two extracts were well treated?

THINGS TO DO

In a group, act the scene at the banquet after the Battle of Poitiers.

Make up a poem about the Black Prince, telling of his good qualities as a knight – or, if you can't manage a poem, pretend to be an old man telling his son about the Prince.

Look again at the love poem. Can you describe in plain, modern English what the lady looked like?

A knight describes his lady

In this poem, written in English but in the style of the French poems of courtly love, a knight talks of the lady he loves. Notice the exaggerated way he describes his despair. In courtly love, it was fashionable to love someone you had no hope of marrying.

Nobly arched her brows appear,
With white between and not too near;
Blissful life she knows.
For loving I am doomed to die.
Her speech, like spice, perfumes the sky,
And seemly is her nose.
So long and lovely is her hair
That when it's falling free and fair
My joy to rapture grows.
A lovely chin, a cheek which glows
With purest white and pink, and shows
The red of flowering rose. . . .
In beaten gold and brightly chased,
Her girdle grips her slender waist;
Its tassel tips her toe.
Besides the emeralds, on it shine
Rubies carved by craftwork fine,
And ranged in row on row . . .

(One of a group of poems by unknown authors, written at the end of the thirteenth or early in the fourteenth century, quoted in *Medieval English Verse*, Penguin Classics, 1964.)

What details in the poem tell you that the knight loves a very rich lady?

Books telling the story of King Arthur were popular from the twelfth century onwards. Here Arthur is shown as an English king (you can see he is wearing the royal arms) fighting an enemy, in a book produced in the thirteenth century.

CAN YOU REMEMBER ?

why King Stephen had to surrender at Lincoln?

who the troubadours were?

what happened at Limoges when the Black Prince took the town?

the different ways in which knights treated different people in war?

CHANGING TIMES

By the end of the fifteenth century, warfare had changed. Battles were no longer won by charges of armed knights. Foot-soldiers were now more important. English archers fighting in France had shown how vulnerable mounted knights were when their horses were shot down. Archers helped Henry V to win the battle of Agincourt in 1415, after which, for a short time, English kings were accepted as kings of France. Soon, though, the French learnt from their mistakes and fought back, helped by a girl, Joan of Arc. Though Joan was burnt to death as a witch (only magic, thought the men, could explain how a woman fought so well!), the French steadily drove the English out of their lands in France. After 1453, only the town of Calais remained in English hands, and the 100 years of raids and battles between English and French armies had ended.

A new weapon had helped to drive the English from France. In 1450 at Formigny in Normandy the French used cannon to batter the English forces. Cannon had been experimented with in the time of Edward III, but at first they were inefficient. By the 1450s there were specialists in artillery who could make better use of the heavy guns. Stone or metal cannon balls propelled by gunpowder could not destroy castle walls but they could batter down gates.

Cannon were very expensive. Only wealthy kings and princes could afford them. It was expensive too to hire soldiers, which was necessary as the old custom of knights giving their service free had died out. Money was the key, and kings got money from wealthy merchants, who then became more important. From the time of Edward I, when English kings called Parliaments to grant taxes, representatives from the towns came to join the 'knights of the shire' in the House of Commons. Though the nobles in the House of Lords and the local knights, too, were still powerful, they were no longer the only people who counted.

Though it was now more difficult for local lords to defy a king, it was still possible if a king was weak. In England, Henry VI was at first a child-king (always a problem – can you think why?) and later mentally ill. The great lords formed parties and fought either for Henry and the royal family of Lancaster, or for the rival family of York. Because one of the Lancastrian badges was a red rose, and one of the Yorkist badges was a white rose, these fifteenth-century civil wars were later nicknamed the 'Wars of the Roses'. Old-style battles, with armoured men riding behind their leaders, were still fought in England, but these followers were now hired 'retainers' rather than devoted vassals. They were often ready to change sides if they could strike a better bargain. Many local knightly families managed to live quietly in their comfortable manor houses, hoping the warring armies would keep away.

The last castles built as strongholds for private families in England and Wales were built well before 1500. Things were different in Scotland and Ireland, where there was more local fighting. Wealthy English families, however, increasingly spent their money on 'castles' like Hever Castle in Kent, which were really luxurious houses with a moat perhaps, and a gatehouse, for security and splendour. It took many years for old ideas and old fashions to die out completely. English kings went on calling themselves kings of France. Sixteenth-century kings like Henry VIII still had suits of armour (you can see his in the Tower of London) and enjoyed jousting in the lists. Now, though, it was all make-believe. Knights and castles already belonged to the past.

What new weapons are in use at this late fifteenth-century siege? Are they likely to make much impression on the strong castle walls?

CHANGING TIMES

Being a knight in the fifteenth century did not always mean being a fighting man. By this time, knighthood was used, as it is today, as a reward for good service or achievement in peace as well as in war. As becoming a knight was expensive, some landowners who qualified chose to pay a fine to the king and stay 'esquires' instead. One family we know a lot about is the Paston family from Norfolk. They kept plenty of their family letters (another sign of change is that more people could now read and write fluently). The Pastons were a family who made money from a peacetime career. William Paston, who first made the family wealthy, was a lawyer. His son John, mentioned below, stayed 'esquire' all his life, but William's grandson, another John, was knighted in 1463.

Disorder in the 1450s

Weak royal government meant that local rivals fought each other and then each side complained that they were the innocent victims. John Paston complained of attacks on himself and his friends by 'Charles Nowell and others', who from their headquarters in a local house,

> **would issue out [set out] at their pleasure, sometimes six, sometimes twelve, sometimes thirty or more, armed, jacked [in a coat of mail] and salleted [helmeted], with bows, arrows, spears and bills [spiked weapons], and over-ride the country and oppress the people and do many horrible and abominable deeds.**
>
> **(Paston Letters, quoted in H. S. Bennett, *The Pastons and their England*, C.U.P., 1922)**

Men like these had such powerful friends that it was almost impossible to bring them to justice. Once, in a quarrel with the Duke of Suffolk, the Duke's men wrecked one of the Pastons' houses.

Castles and tourism

Even ruined castles attract tourists, and parties of students too. (The picture shows a study-group at Tretower, near Abergavenny, in South Wales. You would be able to tell them what kind of a keep they are looking at here.)

A new use for an old castle

Here you can see an old map of Pontefract Castle in Yorkshire. Pontefract dates back to the eleventh century and its Round Tower, on the left, was built in the thirteenth century. This plan belongs to the time of the English Civil War, though: it is dated 1648, when the castle was defended by supporters of Charles I against the troops of the Parliament. You can see the recent fortifications built by the Parliamentary soldiers for the 1648 siege all round the outside of the castle. Like other castles re-used at this time, Pontefract was partly destroyed after its capture by the Parliament, so that it could never be used again.

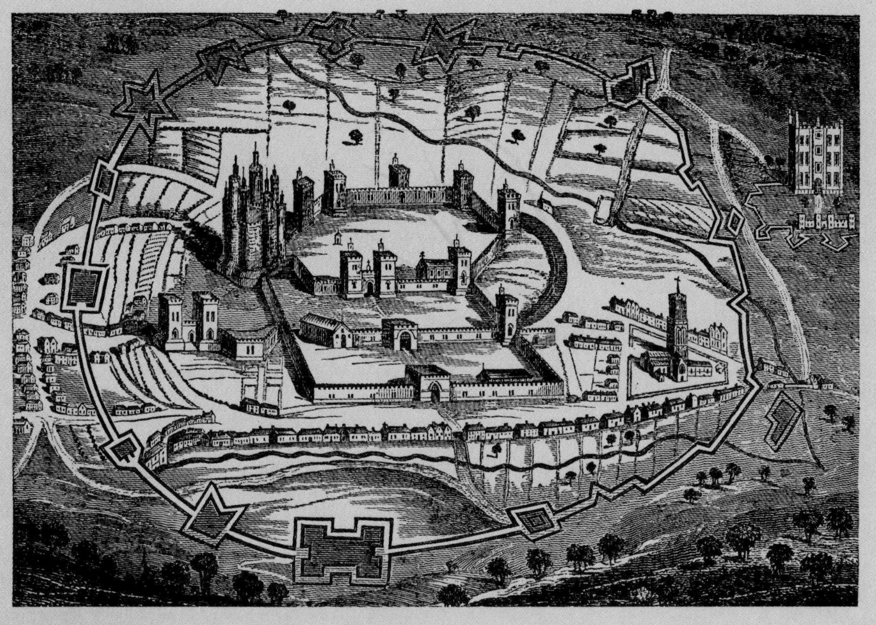

What happened to the castles?

As we have seen, knights and castles did not suddenly disappear. Indeed, some castles are still lived in today. (Do you know of any?) In Victorian times it even became the fashion to build mock castles, or restore old ones. There is a very romantic 'fairy-tale' castle in South Wales called Castell Coch – you can see it from the M4. This was built in the 1870s on the ruins of an old castle.

CAN YOU REMEMBER ?

what kind of homes rich families in England were building for themselves by the end of the fifteenth century?

why the fifteenth-century civil wars are called the 'Wars of the Roses'?

THINGS TO DO

Imagine you are taking a visitor from abroad to see the sights. Look up the nearest castles to your home. Could you easily visit one or more? How would you get there? Plan an excursion and make some notes of the interesting things you would look for: you can find out the details in local history books and guide-books in your public library. Be ready to answer questions from your visitor, who will certainly want to know when the castle was built, and also when it fell out of use (unless, that is, it is still in use today!).

What can you remember?

Do you know

What duties a knightly vassal owed his lord?

Why rulers tried to control castle-building by their vassals?

Why defenders of early castles had to beware of fire?

Why it was useful to build a castle on rock?

Why there are so many castles in Wales?

How fighting in tournaments could benefit a young knight?

What a 'coat of arms' is, and why they were used by knights?

Why hunting was such a popular sport?

In what ways peasant farmers suffered in time of war?

Which people were protected by the code of chivalry?

Why archers using longbows were so useful in a battle?

Any ways in which warfare was changing by the late fifteenth century?

TIME CHART

1066	The Normans conquered England.
1087	William the Conqueror died. His sons William II (1087–1100) and Henry I (1100–35) reigned after him.
1099	The First Crusade captured Jerusalem.
1135	Henry I's nephew, Stephen, became king.
1138	Henry I's daughter and chosen heir, Matilda, launched civil war.
1154	Stephen died, leaving the throne to Matilda's son, Henry.
1154–89	Henry II ruled England and large areas of France (his wife, Eleanor, had inherited Aquitaine in southern France).
1189–99	Richard I ruled England. He went on the Third Crusade, 1189–92.
1204	The king of France conquered Normandy from king John.
1215	King John (1199–1216) granted Magna Carta, a charter of liberties, to rebel barons.
1216	Henry III, a young boy, became king. William Marshal ruled as Regent 1216–19.
1265	(August) Simon de Montfort, a great baron and Henry III's brother-in-law, was killed at the Battle of Evesham. He had led rebellions against Henry.
1272–1307	Edward I ruled England, and conquered Wales. He gave the heir to the throne the title 'Prince of Wales'.
1337	Edward III (1327–77) began a long period of wars with France. He claimed the French throne through his mother.
1346	Battle of Crècy.
1356	Battle of Poitiers. The English captured the French king.
1376	The Black Prince died.
1415	Henry V won the Battle of Agincourt. He died in 1422 and his baby son Henry VI became king of France as well as of England.
1429	The French prince, Charles, supported by Joan of Arc, was crowned king of France.
1431	Joan of Arc was burnt as a witch.
1453	The 100 years or so of fighting in France ended, leaving only Calais still under English rule.
1459–85	The Wars of the Roses: civil war in England. Edward IV of York was king 1461–70 and again 1471–83. Richard III of York was king 1483–85. Then Henry Tudor, the heir of the family of Lancaster, won the Battle of Bosworth and the crown. He married Elizabeth of York and the wars ended.

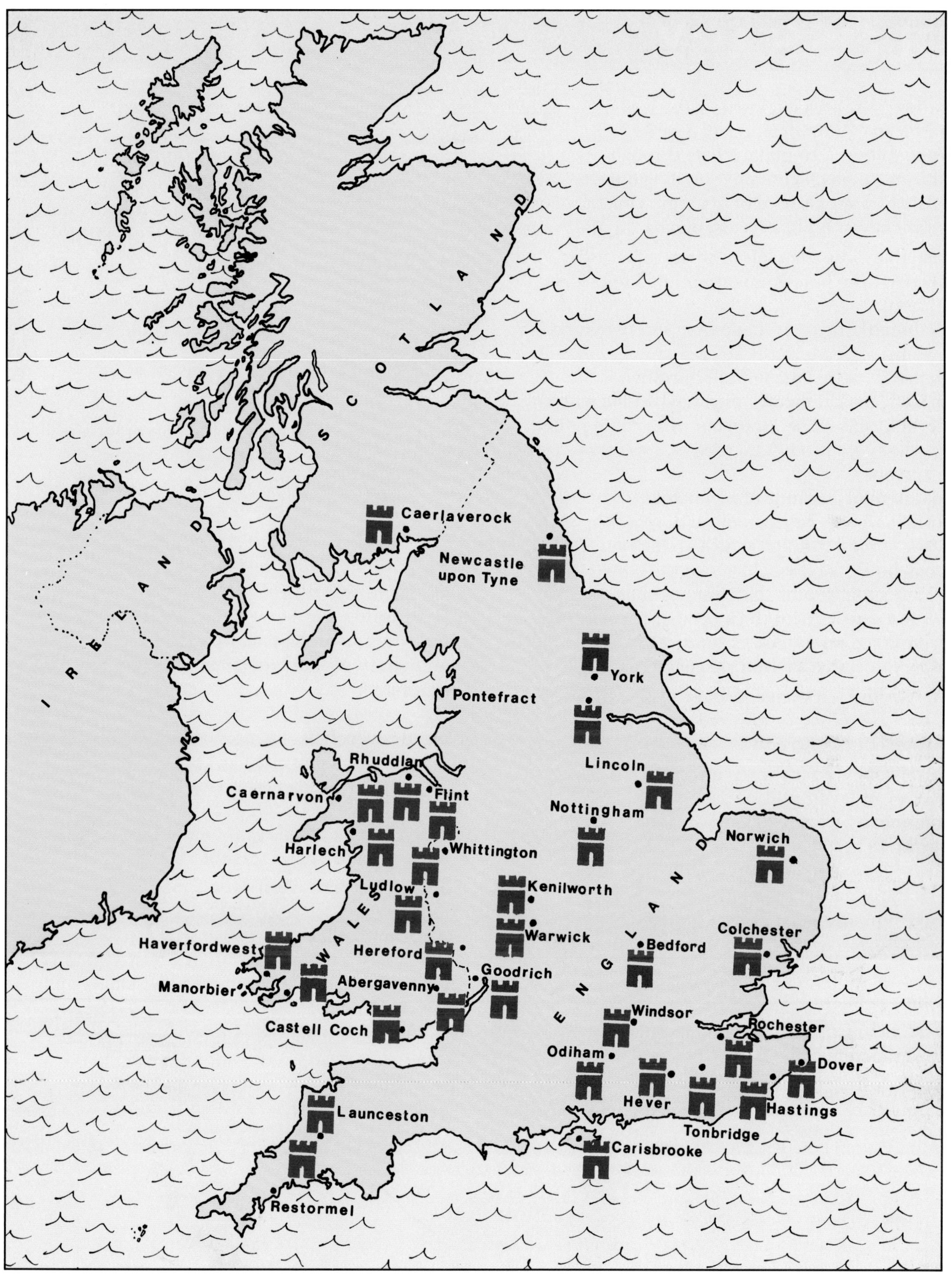
SCOTLAND
IRELAND
WALES
ENGLAND
Caerlaverock
Newcastle upon Tyne
York
Pontefract
Rhuddlan
Caernarvon
Flint
Lincoln
Nottingham
Harlech
Whittington
Norwich
Ludlow
Kenilworth
Warwick
Colchester
Haverfordwest
Hereford
Bedford
Goodrich
Manorbier
Abergavenny
Windsor
Castell Coch
Rochester
Odiham
Dover
Hever
Hastings
Tonbridge
Launceston
Carisbrooke
Restormel

GLOSSARY

bailey the area enclosed by the walls of a castle
barbican outer defences of a castle
bore, to bore to make a hole through
brazier a metal container holding burning fuel
bushel a measurement of grain: a bushel of wheat was 60lb, a bushel of oats was 40lb

castellan the man left in charge of a castle
cavalry the horsemen or mounted soldiers in an army
chainmail armour made from interwoven metal links
charcoal a fuel made from burnt wood
chased, chased metal engraved with a pattern
clerk, king's clerk someone who could write, usually a churchman, used as a secretary or civil servant
coat of mail a tunic of metal links
crenellations battlements with spaces between the stones, through which archers could shoot
cross-bow a bow held across the body, horizontally, and able to shoot bolts (heavy short arrows with thick heads). The bow was mounted on a stock or stump of wood. It was very effective at short range but cumbersome.

drawbridge a bridge, usually over a moat, which could be raised or lowered
dispersed scattered

garde-robe an alcove in a castle wall, used as a privy or lavatory
gatehouse a fortified gateway
girdle a belt
girth a band holding the saddle on a horse: it goes round the horse's stomach

keep the tower or strongpoint of a castle

hall, great hall the main room of a castle or manor house
helm helmet

joust, to joust to fight on horseback in a tournament

lance a weapon used by knights to fight on horseback: it was a long pole with a metal point
lists the area enclosed for a tournament

machicolations holes in a walkway or parapet, jutting over a wall or gate. Missiles or liquids could be dropped through them on to attackers.
mercenary a soldier who fights just for pay, not for a cause or out of loyalty to lord or country
moat a ditch, usually filled with water
motte a castle mound
murder-holes holes in the roof of an entry passage, through which missiles could be dropped

palfrey a small horse or pony
plate gold or silver tableware
plinth a thick slope built at the bottom of a wall
portcullis an iron grating which could be lowered to protect an entrance

quarter a measurement of grain: 8 bushels made one quarter

ransom money paid in exchange for a prisoner
retainer a hired supporter or servant

scale, to scale climb
scutage a fine or tax paid by a knight who did not fight in person when summoned to war by his lord.
sester a measure of wine
sever, to sever cut
shell keep an open circular keep
side-saddle a saddle, especially for women, which makes it possible for a rider to sit sideways on a horse
steward a lord's chief servant

tabard a garment worn over armour or by a herald
tallow animal fat
trestle table a table made up of a board on top of trestles, which can be removed and folded up after a meal

vassal someone who pays homage to a lord in exchange for land, and continues to hold the land while he gives service, usually military service, to the lord.

FURTHER READING

For younger readers

Marjorie Reeves, *The Medieval Castle*, and *The Medieval Knight* Longmans' *Then and There* series.

Jennifer Ruby, *Costume in Context: Medieval Times*, Batsford 1989.

Sheila Sancha, *The Castle Story*, Kestrel, 1979.

For older readers

Maurice Bishop, *The Penguin Book of the Middle Ages*, Penguin 1971.

R. A. Brown, *English Castles*, Batsford 3rd ed. 1976.

John Burke, *Life in the Castle in Medieval England*, Batsford, 1978.

Patrick Cormack, *Castles of Britain*, Peerage Books, 1989.

John Harvey, *The Black Prince and his Age*, Batsford 1976.

Maurice Keen, *Chivalry*, Yale, 1984.

Margaret Wade Labarge, *A Baronial Household of the Thirteenth Century*, Eyre and Spottiswoode, 1965, reprinted Harvester, 1980.

Useful guidebooks

James Forde-Johnston, *A Guide to the Castles of England and Wales*, Constable, 1981.

Ordnance Survey Guide to Castles in Britain, Hamlyn, 1987.

Froissart's Chronicles

Froissart, like Queen Philippa, came from Hainault (then in the Netherlands, now in Northern France). He was a kind of secretary to Philippa in the 1360s but returned from England to the Netherlands when she died in 1368. In about 1369 he began his Chronicles, finishing them about 1400. He died in about 1410. He wrote in French but there is an English paperback translation of selections from the Chronicles published by Penguin.

Acknowledgments

The author and publishers would like to thank the following for permission to reproduce illustrations: Bibliothèque Nationale, Paris for page 22; The Bridgeman Art Library for pages 20, 25, 33, 37, 39, 41 and the frontispiece; The Department of the Environment for page 11; English Heritage for pages 5, 9, 12, 13, 17 and 21; *The Guardian* for page 42; Lambeth Palace Library for page 32; Lighthorne Pictures/Naked City Pictures for page 16; The Royal Commission on the Ancient and Historical Monuments of Scotland for page 10; Matthew Vickers for page 4; The Victoria and Albert Museum for page 27; Geoffrey Wheeler for page 35 and Woodmansterne Ltd for page 36. The map was drawn by Mr M. Chabou.

INDEX

Numbers in **bold type** refer to illustrations.